LOVE IS LOVE

IDEAS AND INSPIRATION
The LGBTQ+ Wedding Book

benton **buckley books**

be bold.

Published by

benton **buckley books**
be bold.

www.bentonbuckleybooks.com

Principal Publisher: Beth Buckley
Associate Publisher: Sheri Lazenby
Art Director: Morganne Stewart
Lead Writer: Lauren Castelli
Editor: Rosalie Wilson
Production Manager: Erica Core

FIRST EDITION

Distributed by Independent Publishers Group
800.888.4741

PUBLISHER'S DATA

Love Is Love
Ideas and Inspiration: The LGBTQ+ Wedding Book

Library of Congress Cataloging-in-Publication Data
has been applied for.
ISBN: 978-0-9964721-8-0

For information about custom editions, special sales, or premium
and corporate books, please contact benton buckley books at
bebold@bentonbuckleybooks.com.

First Printing 2018
10 9 8 7 6 5 4 3 2 1

Excerpt from *Before I Do: A Legal Guide to Marriage, Gay
and Otherwise* - Copyright © 2016 by Elizabeth F. Schwartz.
Reprinted by permission of The New Press.
www.thenewpress.com

TABLE

# of CONTENTS

"we're

lucky

to have the time
we have on the planet and

even

luckier

if we meet someone else to
enjoy the ride with.

Love and be loved."

- Bryan Adams
singer, songwriter, photographer and activist

AN HISTORICAL PERSPECTIVE

No book about marriage for LGBTQ+ people would be complete without at least a basic review of how we have arrived at the freedom to marry nationwide. Marriage equality was won by arduous grassroots and political lobbying, by effective lawyering, and, most of all, by couples willing to share their truths and convince a nation that love is, after all, love.

While many people think that marriage equality started in the 1990s or the 2000s, gays and lesbians were talking about marriage in the 1950s, 1960s, and 1970s. In the interest of space and letting you get to all the fun stuff in this book, we will skip forward to the modern marriage fight. In 1993, three same-sex couples in Hawaii sued to get the right to marry. The Supreme Court of Hawaii ruled in the case of *Baehr v. Lewin* (74 Haw. 530, 852 P.2d 44 [1993], which later became *Baehr v. Miike*) that limiting marriage to heterosexual couples is unconstitutional discrimination. Voters then passed an amendment to the Hawaii constitution defining marriage as between a man and woman, invalidating the court decision. The Hawaii case prompted the concern that an individual state could act to grant equal access to marriage. To address this concern, the United States Congress enacted the Defense of Marriage Act (DOMA) in 1996.

DOMA was a federal law that, until struck down nearly two decades later by the U.S. Supreme Court, defined marriage as only between a man and a woman, denied the federal benefits of marriage to same-sex couples, and allowed states to refuse to recognize otherwise valid marriages of same-sex couples. After DOMA's passage at the federal level, individual states began to pass their own marriage bans through legislation, constitutional amendments, and ballot initiatives until almost all states had their own marriage prohibitions.

Marriage became the vehicle to move the LGBTQ+ rights movement forward. Activists coalesced around this goal, mindful that the right to marry affords couples a dignity that makes it hard to justify discrimination on other grounds. Marriage is a sacred institution and a strong means through which we can get closer to the goal of full equality for our entire community. We began a full-court press, telling our stories and demanding the universal right to enter into marriage to protect ourselves and our relationships.

One of the first national wins in overturning DOMA was by the late, great citizen-activist Edie Windsor. Windsor and her wife, Thea Spyer, were New Yorkers who married in Canada after being together for 41 years. Three years later, Thea passed away. Edie received bills for federal and state estate tax due on Thea's estate. The tax bill was in excess of $638,000. Edie would not owe this estate tax if their marriage had been recognized by the state of New York and the federal government, as spouses can pass an unlimited amount to each other tax-free in life and at death. Edie Windsor was not the only person in this difficult situation. Many people experienced the harms of not having their marriages recognized. Edie sued and won. On appeal, the Supreme Court of the United States agreed that DOMA violated the equal protection and due process provisions of the U.S. Constitution. In 2013 Justice Anthony Kennedy wrote in *Windsor v. United States* (570 U.S. 12): "[*DOMA*] *is invalid, for no legitimate purpose overcomes the purpose and effect to disparage and to injure those whom the State, by its marriage laws, sought to protect in personhood and dignity.*"

With the Supreme Court victory on the federal marriage ban, activists set about undoing the 38 remaining statewide bans against the freedom to marry. Thus began a state-by-state march to full marriage equality throughout the United States, with the powerful wind from the *Windsor* decision at our backs. We began to litigate the individual marriage bans, while LGBTQ+ activists and our many vocal allies continued those conversations about why marriage equality matters, changing hearts and minds of voters, legislators, and judges.

National organizations doing work on LGBTQ+ legal issues and private lawyers teamed up to bring lawsuits in courtroom after courtroom. The victories mounted, with bans being struck down even in some of the most unlikely of states by rather conservative judges who seemed to finally understand that these bans were just pure discrimination and that same-sex marriages hurt absolutely no one and did not infringe on anyone else's rights.

While state after state followed the *Windsor* constitutional analysis, we suffered a few losses. The losses resulted in additional appeals to the United States Supreme Court. A victory in those appeals would mean the remaining 14 states that so far refused to permit or recognize the freedom to marry would have to both issue marriage licenses to same-sex couples and recognize same-sex marriages performed elsewhere. The favorable decision in a consolidated case was released two years to the day after *Windsor.* In the landmark case *Obergefell v. Hodges,* 135 S. Ct. 2584 (2015), the Court found:

> *"It is now clear that the challenged laws burden the liberty of same-sex couples, and it must be further acknowledged that they abridge central precepts of equality. Here the marriage laws enforced by the respondents are in essence unequal: same-sex couples are denied all the benefits afforded to opposite-sex couples and are barred from exercising a fundamental right." (Obergefell, 22)*

It was a sweeping nationwide victory for marriage equality.

Implementing marriage equality is still a work in progress, especially in hostile regions. In some places, marriage, birth, and death certificates have yet to change the terminology they use from "husband" and "wife" to "spouse." Those of us who remain focused on these issues will be busy for many years to come, ensuring that LGBTQ+ people are treated fairly and equitably under the law.

It might seem that the nationwide freedom to marry was achieved at the speed of light, but in fact it was a 45-year-long, painstaking battle fought in every corner of our nation: homes, universities, houses of worship, hospitals, ballot boxes, legislatures, and courts. With this momentum and with the playbook forged by the victors of this battle, we will continue to fight to be free from all discrimination including our goal of winning comprehensive federal discrimination protections in housing, employment, and public accommodations. We are far from done. But oh what a great moment it is to celebrate that love is love!

Elizabeth F. Schwartz
attorney, author, activist

INTRODUCTION

For most couples, the journey from meeting to marriage is complex, full of excitement and struggle, discovery and joy. It's hard to imagine a more powerful experience than the moment the two of you realize you've fallen in love, and that this time it's real. But the decision to commit your lives to one another, to pronounce and celebrate that commitment before and among family and friends, is arguably the most important you'll ever make. For same-sex couples, the decision is even more significant, as until very recently in our country's history, its realization was not possible. Many—and perhaps you're among them—have waited years and even decades for the opportunity to plan a wedding, or even live openly as a couple.

Crimes against gay Americans permeate our history, from the horrors of Stonewall and Pulse nightclubs, to the freedom-stripping strictures of DOMA, and the normalization of hate so prevalent in today's cultural climate only perpetuates the threat to same-sex couples' happiness. For these couples, a wedding represents far more than the actualization of their love; it represents freedom, of overcoming oppressive and antiquated laws and subverting historical paradigms. It's the manifestation of a hard-won victory, of love's ability to break through barriers and overcome hate.

Love Is Love honors and celebrates the vanguards of marriage equality, those who are upending outmoded traditions and redefining what a wedding can and should be. The pages that follow feature the country's top wedding planners, photographers, venues, floral designers, cake makers and tastemakers, all of whom share years of industry experience, a deep-seated passion for their art and, most importantly, an ardent belief that love knows no bounds, and that marriage is everyone's right. Speaking as authorities and from the heart, they present their philosophies and words of wisdom and solidarity to spark ideas and help same-sex couples develop an organic vision for their own weddings.

Even more than a resource, Love Is Love is a passion project, a tribute to the brave individuals who've fought countless oppressors, and to empower others to persist in the fight for validation and equal rights. The images that grace each page speak to the monumental strides we've made in the fight to reclaim marriage, showing same-sex couples dancing and laughing, sharing kisses and vows, and in doing so, writing a new history for us all. Their joy is palpable, it's infectious, and it's a testament to the words of the legendary Edie Windsor: "Marriage is a magic word. And it is magic throughout the world. It has to do with our dignity as human beings, to be who we are openly." *It's high time we made magic.*

Beth Buckley

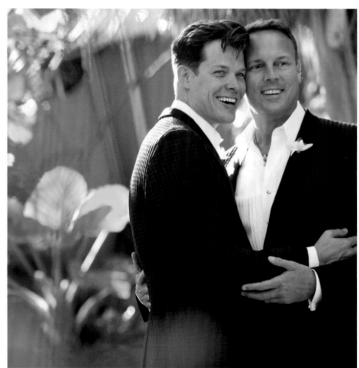

"Real, romantic love is about equal partnership. The best couples take turns lifting each other up — and share spontaneous

KIS

in the kitchen!"
- Bernadette Smith

ANTHONY ABBATIELLO

and

JOHN CHADWICK JOHNSON

request the honor of your presence
to share in their

CELEBRATION OF MARRIAGE

SUNDAY SEPTEMBER 1ST 2013 AT 4 O'CLOCK
cocktails, dinner and dancing to follow

PILGRIM MONUMENT
1 HIGH POLE ROAD
PROVINCETOWN MASSACHUSETTS

RSVP

RSVP

14 STORIES

NEW YORK

Photographs by Kelly Guenther Studio

Photographs by Kelly Guenther Studio

Every couple has a unique and beautiful story to tell, and a truly great wedding is its ultimate expression. I've had the great fortune to help some of the most extraordinary LGBT couples bring their stories to life in celebrations as unforgettable as the loves they celebrate. Though some choose to forgo traditions like dancing with parents and cake cutting, I encourage couples to incorporate a few elements that will give the event a pleasing structure and flow. My clients have incorporated brief drag performances, cabarets, and even aerial acrobatics as conversation starters. Whether timeless, avant-garde, or somewhere in-between, each wedding perfectly captures the couple's original vision and stands as a remarkable testament to true love. ♥ *Bernadette Smith*

"To truly love someone is to be selfless, to put your loved one's needs above your own. It's meeting in the middle even when you don't want to, thinking of that person's feelings before your own.

True love is full of compassion, trust, and faith in one another."

— Natalie Good

Bowtie & Bloom Photography

Brett Hickman Photographers

A GOOD AFFAIR WEDDING
& EVENT PRODUCTION

CALIFORNIA

Brett Hickman Photographers

KLK Photography

Menu

BIANCA & MATTHEW MCRAE

First Course
GAZPACHO, BANYULS VINEGAR, SHRIMP CEVICHE

Second Course
...AD, BANYULS VINAIGRETTE,
...MD CHEDDAR

Photographs by Brett Hickman Photographers

The heart of a wedding is the love that inspires it – a couple who's chosen to join together their lives and to celebrate their union with family and friends. At A Good Affair, we're fueled by this human connection, and we delight in transforming a couple's vision into a unique and memorable event that's a perfect expression of their love. We know that choosing a wedding design firm is a big decision, and my team and I feel very privileged to share our passion for creating unforgettable weddings with same-sex couples throughout Orange County and LA. Each wedding we design begins with a relationship. We take the time to really get to know each couple, learn their likes and dislikes, and earn their trust. Working alongside the couple, we curate every aspect of the event – from the venue selection to reception activities – making sure each perfectly reflects the couple's unique desires and individuality. As I like to say, love is in the details, and those details form the memories that last a lifetime ♥ *Natalie Good*

"When you someone,

you are willing to make sacrifices for that person and their happiness is just as important as your own."

- Alison MacLean

LOVE

ALISON ROSE PHOTOGRAPHY

COLORADO

Photographs by Alison Rose Photography

I consider myself a "wedding photojournalist" because I focus on truly genuine, candid moments. It's important to me that I tell the story of your day so you can remember every special moment, planned or not. You've done tons of work to get here—more obstacles than some people experience—so now it's time to relax and simply enjoy the experience. My bright sense of humor and sentimental nature allow me to truly connect with you on a deeper level, meaning you can relax and simply have fun when I'm taking pictures. This results in authentic shots that never appear fake or forced. If you are happy, it will show through your photographs. There is a special energy when photographing LGBTQ weddings, because they are a celebration of accomplishment, of arriving at your special expression of love. Everyone who comes to these weddings can feel the happiness the couple is experiencing. I also think it's important that future generations know who you were, not just what you looked like. ♥ *Alison MacLean*

"Love is wanting
to spend the rest
of your life
committed to

the happiness
of that one person."

- Wanda Bonner

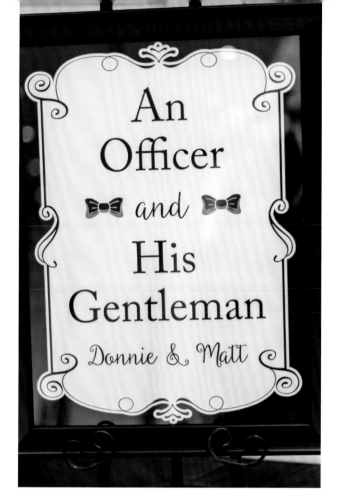

BLUE LINDEN WEDDINGS & EVENTS
COLORADO

58

The best part of any wedding is the celebration of love. Not the beautiful flowers or the matching tablescapes, not the clever signs or cute themes, but the genuine feeling of love and gratitude that a same-sex couple can publicly proclaim, without fear or judgement. Because weddings have traditionally been for heterosexual couples, I encourage same-sex couples to create their own traditions. I may suggest that they don't walk down a center aisle, but rather come in from each side and make equally grand entrances. If the parents are supportive, I suggest that both mom and dad walk with their child. There are also so many ways to incorporate tiny details into the décor as another way to show your guests who you are as a couple. Every couple is different, so the special touches are unique to each wedding. I allow the couple to determine their style and setting because I want the entire day to reflect their vision, not mine. Your wedding day should be everything you want, not what others expect. ♥ *Wanda Bonner*

"We believe that
LOVE
IS LOVE,

and
MARRIAGE
IS MARRIAGE."

- Candy Borales

CANDY + CO.

WASHINGTON, D.C.

Emily Gude Photography

Photographs by Kelly Prizel Photography

The first same-sex wedding we planned, before it became legal, emboldened us to stand alongside those fighting for equality. We encourage each couple to forego tradition for tradition's sake and make their wedding something original; whether it's processing to the theme from *The Golden Girls*, holding a 300-person plated dinner, or reciting vows in an old warehouse. We draw on our unique experiences, connections and vendor relationships to make our clients' visions a reality. The commitment our couples make to each other, in front of their friends and family, is the very definition of love in action. We have a team of passionate women who come from diverse backgrounds and experiences, and our enthusiasm for new ideas and exciting challenges comes through in all we do. We consider ourselves part of a team, working together in harmony, towards our single-minded goal of making each couple's event everything they imagined it could be. ♥ *Candy Borales*

"love does not see color or gender; it sees the soul in which it finds its ultimate sense of comfort and safety.

Find true love,

and you've truly found home." - Mark Kelly

CHICAGO CULTURAL CENTER

ILLINOIS

Photographs by Allison Williams Photography

Though more than a century old, the Chicago Cultural Center is imbued with a sense of currency—it's a venue rooted in history, but always and foremost of the moment, present to and for all who enter. With its two breathtaking glass domes, abundance of architectural opulence and spectacular views of the city's iconic landmarks, the venue is a stunning setting for a wedding. But despite its grandeur, the Center has grown to truly embody its nickname "The People's Palace," serving as original home to Chicago's public library, hosting free performances and art exhibitions, and welcoming hundreds of thousands of visitors annually. Each of our unique event spaces has its own story, but an undeniable sense of home permeates throughout. This welcoming atmosphere draws couples of all race, gender and creed, making the Center the ideal setting for an unforgettable celebration of love. ♥ *Jamey Lundblad*

"Every day *offers a* time for

gratitude." - Todd Gehrke

THE DON CESAR
FLORIDA

Light of the Moon Photography

K and K Photography

Light of the Moon Photography

Light of the Moon Photography

Palm trees, tropical flowers, sugar-fine sand, and uninterrupted views of the Gulf of Mexico make the legendary Don CeSar a welcoming destination. Layer in the luxurious accommodations and world-class Spa Oceana and it's no surprise why many couples choose to get married here and then stay for their honeymoon. With roots to 1928, the landmark hotel is lovingly referred to as Florida's Pink Palace. A palace, indeed, it is well known for its grand celebrations and elevated service. And of course the couple—and their family and friends—will forever connect the joyous occasion with the world-class setting. The Don CeSar's wedding specialists are available to guide all couples through the myriad options for hosting and customizing the wedding events. Many couples like to take advantage of multiple entertainment venues throughout the property, including exchanging vows in the courtyard or on the beach, and then making their way to the hotel's many scenic reception locations—indoors or out. The hotel's classical architecture, beautiful interiors, and natural landscape make exquisite backdrops for photographers to artistically document the wonder of each wedding. ♥ *Todd Gehrke*

"You can follow *old-school* create your own- *that there*

wedding traditions or *the only rule is* are no rules!"

- Heather Vickery

GREATEST EXPECTATIONS

ILLINOIS

I n recent years, I have done more same-sex weddings than straight weddings and even have some local LGBT celebrities as clients. I consider it such an honor to be referred by my peers and vendors to their LGBT friends. What I love most about these weddings is the pure joy that everyone experiences. Many of my couples never imagined being able to marry their love and have a legally recognized union. It is such a beautiful thing. Love means looking beyond yourself, finding ways to listen, support, and lift up your loved ones in any way possible, so we should celebrate when people find that. I enjoy giving my clients a tremendous sense of peace; they know I am a seasoned professional who will guide them throughout the entire process. My mission is to create events and weddings that are meaningful, masterful, and authentic, ones that are inspired by my clients and their ideas and are then guided by my knowledge and expertise. It's a talent for taking people's ideas and turning them into an elevated version of their original vision. ♥ *Heather Vickery*

Photographs by Husar Photography

TRUE
LOVE

is born of vulnerability. Only after you allow yourself to be fully open with one another can you experience the indescribable warmth and happiness that make life worth living."   - Jennifer Burns

HEAVEN EVENT VENUE

FLORIDA

Shane Edwards Photography

eaven Event Venue is the ideal venue for creative-minded couples to bring their wildest dreams to life. We built each space in our unique event center to serve as a blank canvas that can be transformed into any imaginable place—from a romantic Napa vineyard to a hot Miami nightclub. Our contemporary, neutral ambience attracts out-of-the-box thinkers, couples who want to break from tradition and let their personalities take center stage. Same-sex couples are especially adept at designing unconventional, intimate experiences that draw guests in and create lasting memories. One stand-out moment occurred when guests on both sides of the aisle began lighting candles during the ceremony, passing the flame from person to person until reaching the grooms, who then lit each other's, "igniting as one." Sparking these kinds of ideas and helping them shine is our mission at Heaven—and we love what we do! ♥ *Jennifer Burns*

"Every
LOVE

STORY
is *beautiful."*

- Jessica Bordner

JESSICA BORDNER PHOTOGRAPHY

FLORIDA

T he sweetest part of life is witnessing the most important day of a couple's happily ever after. I can't get enough of it—the way a bride glows when she slips into that perfect dress, the way a couple's first kiss as newlyweds fills the room with unspeakable joy. I get to be there to capture these magical moments! I'm the storyteller of this special day. While I stay true to the event's aesthetic and ambience, I always layer in my own editorial perspective and my flair for Southern charm. What I'm after is scrumptious images that convey just the right balance of simplicity and depth. ♥ *Jessica Bordner*

"we love that couples the world over seek out kiawah to tie the knot.

Choosing to marry the love

of your life is the most
important decision
you'll ever make."

- Bryan Hunter

KIAWAH ISLAND GOLF RESORT
SOUTH CAROLINA

Photographs courtesy of Kiawah Island Golf Resort

122

Southern charm meets an idyllic, seaside setting at Kiawah Island Golf Resort, and this unique blend of elegance and nature makes it the perfect destination for celebrations of love. Whether couples are looking for a quiet ceremony on the beach, a magnificent formal reception in the Grand Oaks Ballroom or an intimate cocktail reception in the Ocean Course Clubhouse, our variety of venues and expansive menu of planning and catering services can bring any vision to life. We've helped couples stage casual oyster roasts and barbecues for their rehearsal dinners, organized spa days and cigar bars for wedding parties, designed custom cakes and delivered farewell favors to departing guests. And with five championship golf courses, the stately Sanctuary hotel, abundant recreational activities, 10 miles of beach, intimate villas and historic Charleston a short drive away, Kiawah Resort is the ideal honeymoon retreat. We'll handle the details so the two of you can relax and be fully present in each memorable moment. ♥ *Bryan Hunter*

"We believe that

all love is
perfect."

- Susan Williger

Courtesy of The Langham Huntington, Pasadena

Barnee Photography

THE LANGHAM HUNTINGTON, PASADENA
CALIFORNIA

Courtesy of The Langham Huntington, Pasadena

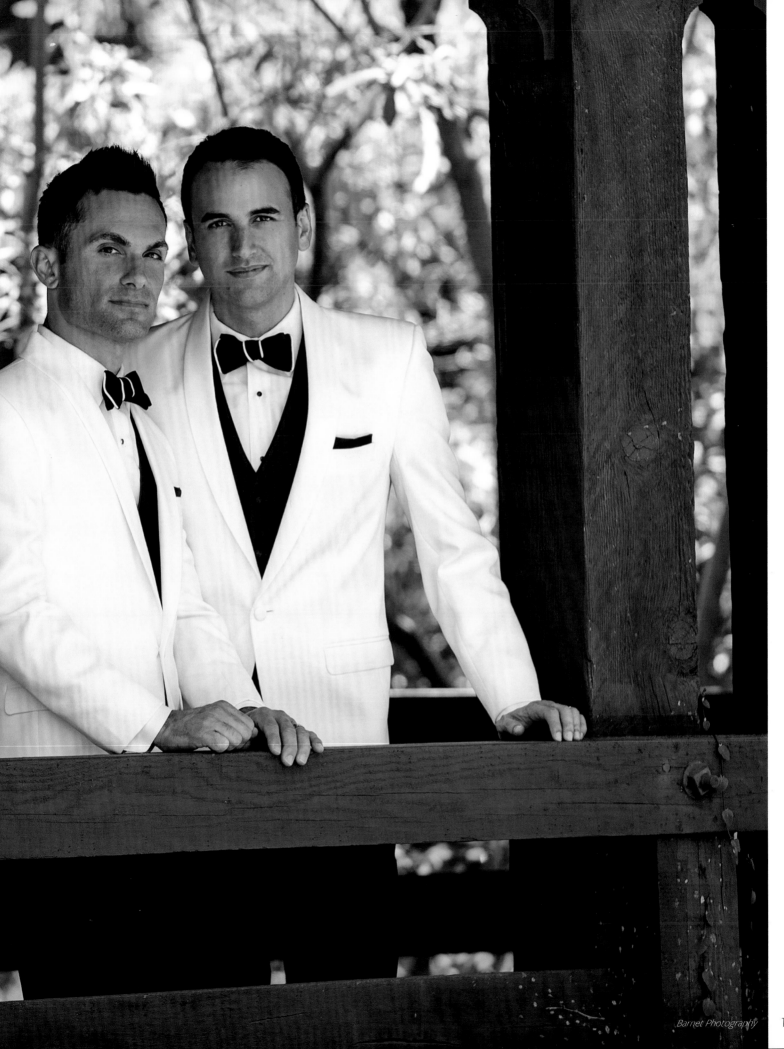

Barnet Photography

Courtesy of The Langham Huntington, Pasadena

Courtesy of The Langham Huntington, Pasadena

Barnet Photography

With three grand ballrooms, three beautifully manicured gardens, and several intimate banquet rooms—all spread out over 23 acres—The Langham Huntington, Pasadena has plenty to offer all couples, no matter what type of ceremony and reception they are seeking. Known as Los Angeles' original getaway, the hotel has great historical significance as it's over 100 years old. Now a globally diverse destination in the heart of Southern California, the hotel specializes in truly personalized events and weddings. The enthusiastic wedding and catering team does all it can to highlight each couple's unique love story and create their perfect celebration, whether intimate or extravagant, traditional or unexpected. The Langham Huntington, Pasadena is also adept at hosting ethnic weddings including Chinese, South Asian, and Middle Eastern weddings, with menus customized to specific regional tastes and preferences. Even the award-winning Chuan Spa, with its cutting-edge skin care technology and treatments inspired by traditional Chinese medicine, is designed to help guests relax and get wedding-ready.
♥ Susan Williger

"Love
is the greatest feeling

anyone can

experience." - Paul Robertson

PAUL ROBERTSON FLORAL DESIGN
CALIFORNIA

PAUL & ROBERTO
5.31.2014
ORGANIC·STRAWBERRY

Photographs by Darren Samuelson

I love to do weddings, no matter the couple, to share in their special day and help bring their vision to life. But there was a time in my life when I never thought I would be able to legally get married, so it is even more important now to recognize the value of love and committed relationships. Weddings are such a wonderful occasion, but the secret to making it less stressful is to gather a great group of vendors. Being located in San Francisco, we have access to one of the most diverse growing regions in the country so I encourage couples to add seasonal color and textures. Couples should incorporate whatever personal touches or traditions that are part of their family or heritage. Seeing the little reminders placed throughout the day help bring it all back to the reason for the day: celebrating with and honoring your family, be they of origin, choice, or both. When you are in love, there are no obstacles too great. Love is definitely a noun and a verb, and today everyone can define it for themselves. ♥ *Paul Robertson*

"Same-sex marriage is a subject close to my heart.

In fact, the first cake I designed for a same-sex wedding was for my dad.

It was such a joy to work with my "bonus" dad on the design, *and even more of an honor to be asked to officiate their wedding.*

I'm very grateful that Růže allows me to add beauty

and joy to other same-sex couples' big day." - Jessica Rose Boutwell

Mary Claire Photography

Andrew Jade Photography

Amy & Jordan Photography

RŮŽE CAKE HOUSE

ARIZONA

Constance Higley

A truly sublime cake is more than a delicious dessert—it's an artful blend of fresh, sustainable ingredients and thoughtful design, a multi-sensory experience meant to be savored and shared. We take this to heart, drawing inspiration from the Southwest's abundant beauty and each couple's personality and style to create beautiful, delectable wedding cakes bursting with local flavor. We love to add elements of the desert landscape, like the heart-shaped prickly pear paddle that tops our signature cake of that name. But true artistry is born of a couple's imagination and taste, as with the cake we created for my dads' wedding. My "bonus" dad's an artist and helped develop the final design—a symbol of their 30-year love. It was the perfect expression of Růže's vision: deeply personal and entirely unforgettable ♥ *Jessica Rose Boutwell*

"to me, to be truly loved means having someone in your life who takes you for what you are,

who knows
you're not perfect,

but loves you anyway.

love is knowing that together you will get through difficult times,

that you'll grow together and support each other."

- Shawn Rabideau

SHAWN RABIDEAU EVENTS & DESIGN
SOUTH CAROLINA

A s a 17-year veteran in the wedding design business, I know that planning a wedding begins with listening to my clients, learning their likes and dislikes, what makes them tick, and creating the blueprint for a wedding that reflects their personalities and makes their style shine. My team and I know the right questions to ask and suggest ideas the couple hasn't yet considered so that the wedding is truly their own, yet exceeds their expectations. As a lifelong rule-breaker, I find planning weddings for same-sex couples especially gratifying because there are no set standards for how the ceremony should go, where each person should stand, or when the vows should be said. We get to make—and break—all the rules, to define a new tradition, create new trends. But more than that, I love working with same-sex couples because they truly embody the meaning of love. Coordinating each element to bring to fruition an idea that for many wasn't even a possibility a decade ago is an overwhelming and emotional experience, and I'm proud to help these couples showcase their love to the world as they finally get the chance to say "I do." ♥ *Shawn Rabideau*

"Love is universal
and should be an

EQUAL

RIGHT

to everyone."
- Julie Shreck

Photographs by Mary Beth Tyson

SIMPLY YOU WEDDINGS
FLORIDA

Photographs by Mary Beth Tyson

Freas Photography

Freas Photography

Blueye Images

In my opinion, same-sex weddings are really no different than other weddings; we are truly one human family and everyone should be able to experience love. With that in mind, same-sex weddings are just as unique and special for the couple and their families. It is two people who love each other, who surround themselves with love, to celebrate love. I find that most of the same-sex events that we do have departed from a lot of the "traditional" wedding needs, and strive to make things more intimate and personalized. Details are a specialty of ours and we encourage our couples to embrace the little things that make you "you," so don't be afraid to personalize whatever aspects of the event might hold special meaning for your story or as a couple. We love to listen to your passions and preferences and discover what matters most to you to make the vision for your special day a reality. Make your wedding unique, but remember that the happiness and love — that little miracle that's visible to others — are by far the highlights of any wedding. ♥ *Julie Shrek*

"To be part of the cultural movement toward understanding and acceptance of all couples is...

it's indescribable."

- Todd Good

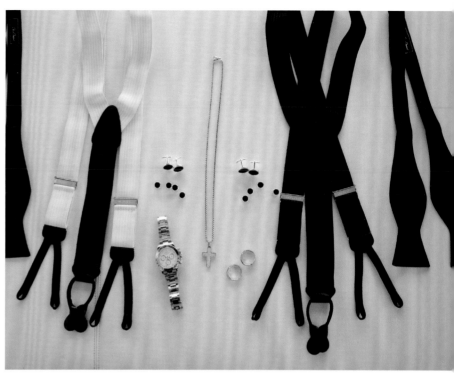

TODD GOOD PHOTOGRAPHY
FLORIDA

Photographs by Todd Good Photography

Photographing weddings is the most rewarding adventure I can imagine. I get to meet new people, experience their joy amongst families and friends, and capture the excitement and emotion of their big day. The images I create depict real moments between couples and those they love—candid, natural, and alive with fun. Viewed alone or together, they tell a story, from the intimacy of the behind-the-scenes preparations, to the vulnerability of the vows, to the unfiltered, goofy antics in the WackyBooth. Essentially, I serve as documentarian, briefly entering a couple's life and celebrating the love they share. I strive to put couples at ease, establishing a bond and earning their trust so they feel comfortable, supported, and free to be themselves. In short, what I do is an act of love—and I love what I do! ♥ *Todd Good*

"**Love** is saying, the **light** in me recognizes, appreciates, and celebrates the light i see and

feel in you."

- Joseph Lanzy

WATERCOLOR INN & RESORT

FLORIDA

arrie Bradshaw, the main character from Sex and the City, once said, "You have to take the tradition and decorate it your way." With same-sex weddings, it's all about creating a unique experience that suits the couple and illustrates what is important to them. For some, that still includes adhering to more traditional wedding aspects, but for others it could mean creating an entirely new experience for them and their guests. With eight ceremony sites available on the property, and a team that's dedicated to ensuring even the tiniest detail is correct, it is possible here to have your day be exactly as you envision it. There is a certain gratitude with our clients, this twinkle in their eyes that says, "thank you for accepting our love and being a part of this dream come true." Love is beautiful, and it's the centerfold of why we do what we do. We finally live in a world where all love is accepted, welcomed, and celebrated. So live in the moment, cherish this dream come true, and then dream bigger. ♥ *Olivia Crawford*

Photographs by Harwell Photography

"I love to create weddings just as fun and layered as the people throwing them. Because –

no matter what you're celebrating, the best parties feel like magic."

- Tabitha Abercrombie

WINSTON & MAIN

CALIFORNIA

Square Productions

Square Productions

WAVE &
CHEER
THE BRIDES
ARE NEAR!

Square Productions

Evangeline Lane Photography

J Wiley Photography

Evangeline Lane Photography

Evangeline Lane Photography

You're engaged! You've picked a date, you've got your guest list, and you may even have a venue secured. The two of you are planning your wedding, a day to honor each other, celebrate together, and flaunt your unique, wild, and wonderful selves. You've got a-million-and-one ideas but bringing them to life seems impossible, right? Wrong! I've totally got you. In fact, I started Winston & Main to help modern couples create bold, stylish, and deeply personal weddings, as beautiful and unique as they are. Once I've gotten to know you over coffee or cocktails, I get to work crafting a design concept complete with color and fabric swatches, sketches, and images to help shape and solidify your vision. I then create custom décor, organically inspired floral arrangements, and memorable statement pieces as sparkly and unique as you are. From backdrops to tabletops, and everything in between, I design and create a vision that builds a whole world around the love you're celebrating. ♥ *Tabitha Abercrombie*

An Excerpt

from "BEFORE I DO: A Legal Guide to *Marriage*, Gay and Otherwise"

Weddings serve a broader purpose than giving you reason to throw a big party or put together an epic wish list for new dishes and linens to start off a domestic life together. Part of the larger point of a wedding is to stand up in the presence of your loved ones as they bear witness to your vows and lifetime pledges to one another. The wedding ceremony brings families and communities together in a public affirmation of the relationship between the spouses. The Supreme Court of the United States was conscious of this and, in the Windsor decision, held that the Defense of Marriage Act (DOMA) deprived same-sex couples of the fundamental right to "affirm their commitment to one another before their children, their family, their friends, and their community."

In a wedding, the couple implicitly asks for support from their community when times get tough. Especially in our transient society, having a broad network of friends and family can relieve your spouse of the pressure of being your sole source of support. No one person can be your "everything." Moreover, no marriage is without its challenges. The hope is that the people who attend your wedding will buttress the union when you hit a bumpy patch in the road. Either you or the officiant might announce that specific request during the ceremony, making the expectation clear that you hope your guests will help strengthen the relationship, not undermine it.

Do not be afraid to color outside the lines while still respecting the traditions that are important to you. Give yourself license to reimagine some of the wedding rituals to best suit you and your bride or groom. For example, you might not both be lucky enough to have parents to walk you down the aisle. Consider giving that honor to a mentor or another dear soul who has been particularly supportive of you on your journey. Or maybe you would rather walk each other down the aisle instead, as a sign of your empowerment as a couple and as a break from the heterocentric and paternalistic convention that says a grown-up needs to be "given away."

And do announce your marriage! By having your marriage announced on social media sites or in the newsletters for your alma maters, religious institutions, and the like, you are being role models to other LGBT people, single or coupled, who still live with the fear of stigma.. For many couples who have spent years calling our intended lifetime partners our "friends" or some other euphemism, it can be incredibly empowering to step into the sunshine and declare our love and commitment.

It is a great gift to your hetero family and friends to give them the opportunity to come out themselves about their support of marriage equality. The value of educating them cannot be overestimated. It is the difference between intellectually believing and actually seeing. Marriage equality may now be the law of the land, but there is still resistance, largely among those who are less familiar with the LGBT community and our families. Here's to your big day and to your role in broadening cultural acceptance of marriage equality!

Elizabeth F. Schwartz
attorney, author, activist

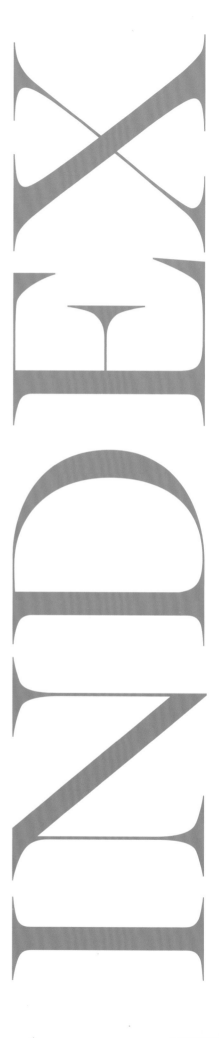

INDEX

SPECIAL THANKS

We would like to thank all the photographers who contributed to this book.

1001 Angles Photography
1001angles.com

Abby Hart Photo
blog.abbyhartphoto.com

Alison Rose Photography
aroseweddings.photography

Allison Maginn Photography
allisonmaginn.com

Allison Williams Photography
allisonwilliamsphoto.com

Amy & Jordan Photography
amyandjordan.com

Andrew Jade Photography
andrewjadephoto.com

Barnet Photography
barnetphotography.com

Best Photography
joshandrachelbest.com

Blueye Images
blueyeimages.com

Bowtie & Bloom Photography
bowtieandbloom.com

Brett Hickman Photographers
bretthickman.com

Constance Higley
constancehigley.com

Darren Samuelson
darrensamuelson.com

Elevate Photography
elevatephotography.com

Emily Gude Photography
egudephoto.com

Eternal Light
eternal-lightphotography.com

Evangeline Lane Photography
evangelinelane.com

Freas Photography
fotobyfreas.com

Harwell Photography
harwellphotography.com

Hartley Aerial Services
wadehartley.com

Husar Photography
husarphotography.com

J Wiley Photography
jwileyphotography.com

Jessica Bordner Photography
jessicabordner.com

K and K Photography
kandkphotography.com

Kate McElwee Photography
katemcelweephotography.com

Kathy Thomas Photography
kathythomasphotography.com

Kelly Guenther Studio
kellyguentherstudio.com

Kelly Prizel Photography
kellyprizel.com

KLK Photography
klkphotography.com

Light of the Moon Photography
lightofthemoonphotography.com

Lock + Land Photography
lock-land.com

Maring Visuals
maringvisuals.com

Mary Beth Tyson Photography
marybethtyson.com

Mary Claire Photography
maryclaire-photography.com

Next Exit Photography
nextexitphotography.com

Romi Burianova
romiburian.com

Shane Edwards Photography
shaneedwardsphotography.com

Square Productions
squareproductions.com

Sugar Pop Films
sugarpopfilms.com

Todd Good Photography
toddgood.com

Unashamed Imaging
unashamedimaging.com

Victoria Gold Photography
victoriagoldphotography.com

Wild and Wonderful Photography
wildandwonderfulphotographywv.com

LGBTQ+ ASSOCIATIONS

Affirmation
affirmation.org

American Civil Liberties Union
aclu.org

Association of Welcoming
and Affirming Baptists
awab.org

DignityUSA
dignityusa.org

Equality Federation
equalityfederation.org

Family Equality Council
familyequality.org

Fellowship of Reconciling Pentecostals
International
rpifellowship.com

Freedom for All Americans
freedomforallamericans.org

Gay and Lesbian Alliance
Against Defamation (GLAAD)
glaad.org

GLBTQ Legal Advocates
and Defenders (GLAD)
glad.org

Gay, Lesbian, and Straight
Education Network (GLSEN)
glsen.org

Human Rights Campaign
hrc.org

Immigration Equality
immigrationequality.org

Keshet
keshetonline.org

Lambda Legal
lambdalegal.org

Marriage Equality FAQ
marriageequalityfacts.org

Metropolitan Community Churches
mcchurch.org

More Light Presbyterians
mlp.org

Muslims for Progressive Values
mpvusa.org

National Center for Lesbian Rights
nclrights.org

National Center for Transgender Equality
transequality.org

National LGBTQ Task Force
thetaskforce.org

National LGBT Bar Association
lgbtbar.org

Outserve/SLDN
(Servicemembers Legal Defense Network)
outserve-sldn.org

PFLAG
pflag.org

ReconcilingWorks: Lutherans
for Full Participation
reconcilingworks.org

Room for All
roomforall.com

Services and Advocacy
for LGBT Elders (SAGE)
sageusa.org

Servicemembers, Partners, Allies for
Respect and Tolerance for All (SPART*A)
spartapride.org

Transgender Law Center
transgenderlawcenter.org

Transgender Legal Defense
and Education Fund
transgenderlegal.org

Unitarian Universalist Association
uua.org